WISCONSIN

WISCONSIN

The Spirit of America

Text by Joanne Trestrail

Abrams, New York

This series was originated by Walking Stick Press, San Francisco
Series Designer: Linda Herman; Series Editor: Diana Landau

Editor: Nicole Columbus
Designer: Ana Rogers

Photo research: Laurie Platt Winfrey, Van Bucher, Carousel Research, Inc.

Page 1: *Evening Holsteins* by Daniel Gerhartz, n.d. *Courtesy of the artist*
Page 2: *Wisconsin Farm Scene* by John Steuart Curry, 1941. *Elvehjem Museum of Art, University of Wisconsin*

Library of Congress Cataloguing-in-Publication Data
Trestail, Joanne.
  Wisconsin : the spirit of America / text by Joanne Trestail.
    p.   cm.
  ISBN 10: 0–8109–5573–3
  ISBN 13: 978–0–8109–5573–8
  1. Wisconsin—Civilization—Miscellanea.   2. Wisconsin—Description and
  travel—Miscellanea.   3. Wisconsin—Pictorial works.   I. Title.

F581 .T74 2001
977.5—dc21   2001018825

Printed and bound in China
10 9 8 7 6 5 4 3

HNA ■■■■■
harry n. abrams, inc.
a subsidiary of La Martinière Groupe

115 West 18th Street
New York, NY 10011
www.hnabooks.com

A couple and child pose with their crops. *State Historical Society of Wisconsin*

CONTENTS

Oh, that glorious Wisconsin wilderness! Everything new and pure in the very prime of the spring....

John Muir, The Story of My Boyhood and Youth, 1913

Harvest Time by Lois Ireland, 1944. Collection of Mr. and Mrs. John Bolz

Picture-perfect farmland is only part of the picture in Wisconsin. Certainly, vast stretches in the southern part of the state still resemble illustrations in children's books—snug-looking family farms, Holsteins grazing in contentment. And many small towns continue to look like small towns, resisting chain-retailer homogenization.

But there are other Wisconsins. The North Woods world of muskie fishing, hunting, and snowmobiling is its own place. Northerners glance at their outdoor thermometers in January, see that it's five below zero, and think: "I've got to get out there." They know how to bundle up.

Echoes of early immigration are everywhere—in architecture and ethnic festivals, bakeries and souvenir shops. But not everyone is of European descent. The state also has significant communities of Native Americans, African Americans, Hispanics, and Asians, mostly Laotian Hmong.

The state has two major urban centers. Milwaukee, with about 600,000 people, is the larger and more ethnically mixed. The Lake Michigan metropolis has a beery, blue-collar past, a tradition of social reform, and a vibrant cultural scene. In Madison, the capital and home of the University of Wisconsin's main campus, unreconstructed hippies feel less out of place than they might elsewhere. A hotbed of student activism in the late 1960s and early 1970s, the city combines academic cosmopolitanism and state-government buzz with pastoral pleasures.

Place names in Wisconsin reflect its first inhabitants. Indian words are common, although their derivations are often uncertain. They are easy to pronounce when you know how. (Tip on "Oconomowoc": Accent the "con.") Explorers left behind French names for towns and rivers but no one to guard their pronunciations. Prairie du Chien became "Prare doo sheen," Fond du Lac "Fonn delack."

Other Wisconsinisms: Thirsty? A local may point you in the direction of the nearest "bubbler." It's a water fountain. Hungry? Try a supper club. Membership is not required. In Wisconsin, a supper club is a restaurant where prime rib and home-style chicken are menu fixtures; Friday night fish fries and pre-meal relish trays are de rigueur. A helping of cole slaw, pickled beets, three-bean salad, and a dinner roll should tide you over till your entrée comes.

About eating as about other matters Wisconsinites are boldly unself-conscious. If you want your brat on a buttered roll, nobody's going to stop you. Butter rules!

Which brings us to cheese. More so even than brats and beer, Wisconsin is

Relaxing in 1890s Wisconsin. *State Historical Society of Wisconsin*

A 1930s carved and painted wood sturgeon, with metal attachments, by Edward Frerks, Sr. *Milwaukee Art Museum, Michael and Julie Hall Collection*

about cheese. Do Packer fans wear foam rubber brats on their heads? No. They wear cheese. In Wisconsin, a meal in a nice restaurant may well include cheese soup, cheese potatoes, and apple pie with cheese. In a private home, expect to be offered thick slices of mild Colby (invented in Colby, Wisconsin) as a between-meals snack.

It's an unnervous state, which is not to say bored or boring. Idiosyncrasies flourish without demanding a national stage (Joe McCarthy aside). Independent politics is a tradition. So is independent-minded entrepreneurship, covering everything from Tommy Bartlett-style Dells hucksterism to Pleasant Rowland's American Girl doll company.

Creativity is another tradition. Who can explain the abundance of large-scale, outdoor "outsider" art in Wisconsin? It's as much a part of the landscape as Frank Lloyd Wright's graceful Taliesin and might draw the same, enigmatic half-compliment from Wisconsinites: "Well, that's different."

Which is not to say they don't like it, or aren't glad to be there. 🐄

WISCONSIN

"The Badger State"
30th State

Date of Statehood
MAY 29, 1848

Capital
MADISON

Tree
SUGAR MAPLE

Bird
ROBIN

Flower
WOOD VIOLET

Soil
ANTIGO SILT LOAM

Grain
CORN

Dance
POLKA

"Forward"

State motto

Wisconsin's history-in-a-nutshell flag features symbols of mining, agriculture, manufacturing, and navigation. It also shows a

Robin and wood violet

badger, the state animal, not to be confused with the state wildlife animal (white-tailed deer) or domestic animal (dairy cow). "The Badger State" is an unofficial nickname (as is "America's Dairyland," the license-plate slogan), and "badger" is itself a nickname. Lead miners who swarmed into southwestern Wisconsin around 1830 were called badgers, disparagingly, because they took shelter in abandoned mine shafts and burrows dug into hillsides. As the name lost its sting, the feisty animal became an informal state symbol, finding further celebrity as the mascot of the University of Wisconsin-Madison, Bucky Badger.

"On, Wisconsin"

When "On, Wisconsin" was named state song in 1959, many different lyrics existed. By law, the official text is:

On, Wisconsin! On, Wisconsin!
Grand old badger state!
We, thy loyal sons and daughters,
Hail thee, good and great.
On, Wisconsin! On, Wisconsin!
Champion of the right,
"Forward" our motto—
God will give thee might!

"On, Wisconsin" was originally a college fight song. William Purdy wrote it in 1909 as an entry in a Minnesota contest for a new university football song, but was persuaded by his collaborator on the lyrics, Carl Beck, to dedicate the song to the University of Wisconsin instead.

The state capitol in Madison. *Photo Zane Williams. Below left:* **Badger (***Taxidea taxus***).** *Photo Stephen Krasemann/ Photo Researchers. Below:* **Wood violet and trillium in Door County.** *Photo Zane Williams*

The American water spaniel is bred to hunt and retrieve all kinds of game. It can retrieve birds as large as Canada geese and leap back into a fishing boat without tipping it over. *Photo Alan and Sandy Carey/Photo Researchers Below:* Milk, the state beverage. *Photo Phillip Hayson/Photo Researchers*

Born to Fetch

One of only five dog breeds indigenous to the United States and the only one native to Wisconsin, the American water spaniel was named state dog in 1985. It is known for its intelligence, merry disposition, and practical skill as a hunting dog. The breed was developed for waterfowling from small boats, but it also is a popular household pet and watchdog. It is medium in size (usually 25 to 45 pounds) and has a curly, dark brown coat.

The White Stuff

Some people are surprised to hear that the state beverage isn't golden and alcoholic. It's the other one—milk. Although Wisconsin no longer leads the nation in dairying, having been bypassed by California in 1993, it still puts out milk in great quantity and produces a third of the nation's cheese.

Some Fish

In many parts of Wisconsin, rec rooms are considered unfinished if they don't have a taxidermied muskie, the state fish, hanging over the fireplace. The powerful, fast-swimming muskellunge, found in more than 700 lakes in the state, inspires Ahab-like obsession among sports fishermen. Torpedo-shaped, with rock-hard flesh, the mighty muskie has the largest canine teeth of any freshwater fish. It has been known to eat ducks and even other muskie. The National Freshwater Fishing Hall of Fame in Hayward is housed in a 143½-foot-long, 4½-story fiberglass building in the shape of a muskie.

"WE FINALLY HOOKED AND LANDED OLD 'CHIN WHISKERED Charlie'. . . 69 pounds, 11 ounces, 5 feet 3½ inches long."

Louie Spray, credited with catching the world record muskie in the Chippewa Flowage on October 20, 1949

The National Freshwater Fishing Hall of Fame in Hayward. *Photo Zane Williams*

A picnic isn't a picnic without bratwurst, a.k.a. brats (rhymes with "spots") on the grill. Even in this sausage-mad part of the country, where Native Americans stuffed deer intestines with meat and herbs long before German immigrants arrived, brats reign supreme. Wisconsin brats are made with pork and natural casings; texture and spices vary from butcher to butcher. Purists dress brats with mustard and eschew other condiments. Sheboygan, the Bratwurst Capital of the World, hosts a Bratwurst Days festival every August.

WISCONSIN MILESTONES

1000 A.D. Oneota Indian villages established around Green Bay, Lake Winnebago, Lake Koshkonong, and La Crosse.

1200s Major community at Aztalan is abandoned.

1634 First European in area, Jean Nicolet, explores western Great Lakes.

1673 Jacques Marquette and Louis Jolliet discover Upper Mississippi River.

1716 French attack Fox Indian village at Lake Buttes des Morts, gain control of fur trade.

1745 Charles Langlade, son of a French father and Ottawa mother, builds first farm in upper Midwest, near Green Bay.

1754–63 Wisconsin Indians, led by Langlade, fight British and British-American colonists in French and Indian War.

1763 With Treaty of Paris, France cedes all lands east of Mississippi River; Wisconsin becomes part of British colonial territory.

1783 Second Treaty of Paris. Wisconsin becomes territory of the United States.

1822 Oneida, Stockbridge Munsee, and Brothertown Indians move to Wisconsin from eastern U.S.; lead mining begins in southwestern part of state.

1825 Erie Canal completed, boosting immigration.

1831 Lucius Lyon begins public land survey in Wisconsin.

1832 Black Hawk War ends Native American resistance to settlers in state.

1836 Territory of Wisconsin is created by Congress; Madison established as capital.

1838 University of the Territory of Wisconsin founded.

1840s Norwegians arrive in large numbers in Koshkonong area.

1848 Wisconsin becomes 30th state; German immigration begins in earnest; *Milwaukee Sentinel & Gazette* published on first paper made in state.

1851 First railroad opens, linking Milwaukee and Waukesha; first state fair held at Janesville.

1854 Wisconsin abolitionists defy Fugitive Slave Act; Republican Party formed in Ripon.

1856 Margarethe Schurz opens first American kindergarten in Watertown.

1865 96,000 Wisconsin soldiers serve in Civil War; 12,216 die in conflict.

1868 Milwaukee newspaperman Christopher Sholes patents first practical typewriter.

1871 Fire levels town of Peshtigo; 1,200 die.

1872 Wisconsin Dairyman's Association founded in Watertown.

1886 Workers strike for eight-hour work day in Bay View—five die in confrontation with militia.

1890 First souvenir shops appear in Wisconsin Dells.

1899 Lumbering boom in northern Wisconsin; first muskellunge stocking efforts in state lakes.

1901 Reformer Robert M. LaFollette, Sr., begins first of two terms as governor.

1907 Socialist administration elected in Milwaukee.

1909 Ole Evinrude designs first outboard motor.

1911 Frank Lloyd Wright begins working and living at Taliesin, near Spring Green.

1917 African Americans from rural South come to Wisconsin in large numbers.

1919 Wisconsin legislature ratifies 19th Amendment (women's suffrage), first state to deliver ratification to Congress.

1924 Robert M. LaFollette, Sr., runs for president, wins Wisconsin; Carl Eliason invents snowmobile.

1932 Wisconsin enacts first unemployment-compensation law in U.S.

1933 Dairy farmers strike, protesting low prices.

1953 Braves move from Boston to Milwaukee; Hank Aaron signs contract with the Milwaukee Braves.

1959 St. Lawrence Seaway opens, bringing increased traffic to Wisconsin ports; Vince Lombardi becomes coach of Green Bay Packers.

1966 Braves and Aaron move to Atlanta.

1967 Antiwar protests at UW-Madison; Green Bay Packers win first Super Bowl ever played, beating Kansas City Chiefs.

1970 Milwaukee Brewers return major-league baseball to state.

1975 Menominee tribe regains federal recognition.

1980 Madison speed skater Eric Heiden wins five gold medals at Winter Olympics.

1987 State lottery instituted.

1996 Wisconsin Works program enacted.

Hillside and valley in Richland County. *Photo Zane Williams*

Wisconsin's peaceful topography belies the geological violence of its origins. During the last glacial advance, known as the Wisconsin period, about two-thirds of the state was covered with a thick, scouring mass of ice. Its retreat 10,000 years ago left behind carved rock and rolling hills where mountains once stood. Mounds of till, or moraines, contain boulders and sediments from far-off places. Diamonds that might be from the Hudson Bay area have been found in some moraines.

In the southern part of the state, the quality of the soil and temperate weather make agriculture prosper. Where dairying and traditional crops such as corn and alfalfa are less viable, enterprising farmers have turned to specialty products, including cranberries and ginseng. In the north, hardwood and evergreen forests define the view. Wisconsin's terrain holds dramatic surprises, from the elaborate natural sculpture of the Dells to rocky Door Peninsula between Lake Michigan and Green Bay. Most unexpectedly, for the Midwest, are the palisades and waterfalls along the Lake Superior coast and the pastel sandstone Apostle Islands just off it.

Wisconsin Landscape by John Steuart Curry, 1938–39. *Courtesy The Metropolitan Museum of Art*

Water World

The Upper Mississippi, near Fountain City. *Opposite:* The Lake Michigan shoreline, at Cave Point Country Park in Door County. *Both, Photo Zane Williams*

With two Great Lakes and the Mississippi River edging it, Wisconsin has access to big water in three different directions. It also has more than 15,000 lakes, nearly half of them unnamed. And it has the mighty, 430-mile-long Wisconsin River running southward from the Michigan boundary to near Madison, where it hooks west toward the Mississippi. Its flow is regulated by reservoirs; other rivers, including the St. Croix, the Namekagon, the Wolf, and the Pike, are wild. Wisconsin has so many lakes, even its cities are full of them: Madison has four within its borders.

Recreational waters help make tourism the third-largest business in the state (after agriculture and manufacturing). Door County, Lake Geneva, and the Dells draw thousands of boaters and swimmers in summer. Lakes Michigan and Superior attract serious sports fishermen with their muscular lake trout and king and coho salmon. But hard work is taking place as well; Wisconsin ports handle more than a quarter of all domestic freight tonnage on the Great Lakes.

Winging It

Wetlands all over the state draw gaggles of birds and birders. The 32,000-acre Horicon Marsh, west of Milwaukee, was established as a habitat for migrating and nesting ducks but also has become a stopover for more than 200,000 Canada geese every spring and fall. The state has hundreds of eagle nesting sites; the magnificent birds are especially observable along the Mississippi River and the Lower Wisconsin State Riverway. The Upper Mississippi River National Wildlife and Fish Refuge is home or nesting area to more than 250 species of birds.

"THERE ARE ASPECTS OF WILDERNESS STILL, AT ITS HEADWATERS as well as near its mouth: in the wooded islands, the hill slopes, the forest country—and a kind of nostalgic wildness in its name: Wisconsin."

August Derleth, The Wisconsin: River of a Thousand Isles

Timber!

Lush woods cover nearly half of Wisconsin.
Photo Zane Williams

To the earliest non-native Americans, the natural resources of their new country, its boundaries ever expanding, seemed inexhaustible. Before white settlement, forest covered 85% of what is now Wisconsin. Here was timber for the taking, enough pine, oak, maple, cedar, spruce, and tamarack to keep the young nation supplied with barrels and broom handles

forever. Unchecked lumbering made Wisconsin the country's largest timber producer by 1870, with a billion board feet passing through the state's mills each year. The North Woods rang all winter with the sound of trees being felled, dragged to rivers' edges by horse-drawn sleds, then

Workers felled trees, and oxen moved them out. Wisconsin was the nation's largest timber producer by 1870.
State Historical Society of Wisconsin

floated downstream to sawmills when the spring thaw came. But the end came sooner than expected. By 1920, its forests depleted, much of Wisconsin was a cut-over wasteland.

The trees that once again cover nearly half the state are the result of natural regrowth and reforestation. Many are grown specifically for papermaking, an industry in which Wisconsin leads the nation. Today's manufacturers, their plants concentrated around Wisconsin Rapids, Appleton, and Wausau, make everything from cardboard boxes to tea bags.

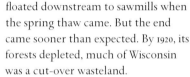

"The great, dark trees of the Big Woods

stood all around the house, and beyond them were other trees and beyond them were more trees. As far as a man could go to the north in a day, or a week, or a whole month, there was nothing but woods."

Laura Ingalls Wilder, Little House in the Big Woods, *1932*

Earliest Peoples

The first Wisconsinites were nomadic Paleo-Indians who
passed through about 11,000 B.C. They were followed a few
thousand years later by people who mined and melted cop-
per, remnants of which have been found near Green Bay and
along the Fox River. Then came the Woodland people, who
left pieces of pottery and effigy mounds in the shapes of animals. From about 200 B.C. to A.D. 500, the Hopewell people
farmed along rivers in the southwestern part of the state. By
approximately 1000 A.D. they had been replaced by the Missis-

sippian culture, probably the first people in the area to hunt with bows and arrows. Some archaeologists think their civilization extended to Mexico or even beyond.

The connection between the Mississippians and the Native Americans of written history is not clear, but the Indians encountered by European fur traders early in the 17th century were mostly Ho Chunk (Winnebago), Ojibwe (Chippewa), and Iroquois. By 1616, Ottawa and Huron had arrived from the Northeast and set up trading centers, eager to do business with the Europeans.

Ancient Secrets

A mystery lurks in the waters of Rock Lake, only a few miles from Aztalan State Park's flat-topped Mississippian pyramid mounds. Structures on the lake bottom are thought by some to be ruined pyramids and ceremonial constructions; others dismiss them as natural glacial debris. The lake also contains a small, unusual island apparently molded of coiled earth, serpent-like, on which a number of ancient artifacts have been found.

The French Arrive

In 1634, explorer Jean Nicolet and his party became the first Europeans on the western shore of Lake Michigan, landing near what is now the city of Green Bay. Other French, mostly fur traders and priests, soon followed. Relations between them and the Native Americans, engaged in territorial disputes of their own, were sometimes guardedly friendly, sometimes rough. By the mid-18th century Ottawa had arrived from Canada, Potawatomi and Sauk from Michigan. Wisconsin's first permanent "European" settler, Charles Langlade, was, in fact, the son of an Ottawa mother and a French father. In 1763 the French lost control of territory that included Wisconsin in the French and Indian War, signing over large tracts to Great Britain.

In 1825, the still-new U.S. government signed the Treaty of Prairie du Chien, getting local tribes to establish boundaries

Nicolet's Landing by Edwin Willard Deming, n.d. When French explorer Jean Nicolet landed near Green Bay in 1634, he walked ashore in Chinese silk robes brandishing pistols, in the mistaken belief that the Winnebago could show him a passage to Asia. *State Historical Society of Wisconsin*

to land they claimed along the Mississippi. Two years later, a skirmish between Winnebago and area settlers led to the cession of the district to the government, and even more Native Americans were forced west. In 1832, warrior-leader Black Hawk rallied Fox and

Sauk, who had been displaced to Iowa, to try to reclaim their lands in Illinois. Pushed north up the Rock River into Wisconsin, the beleaguered band engaged in one final, losing battle with militia brigades led by Gen. Henry Atkinson. The bloody Black Hawk War marked the end of local Indian resistance to European settlement.

Black Hawk held: In reason
land cannot be sold,
only things to be carried away,
and I am old.

Young Lincoln's general moved,
pawpaw in bloom,
and to this day, Black Hawk,
reason has small room.

Lorine Niedecker, untitled poem included in
The Collected Poems (1936–1966)

Ball Play of the Women, Prairie du Chien by George Catlin, 1835–36. National Museum of American Art, Smithsonian Institution, Washington, D.C./Art Resource Left: Chief Black Hawk. State Historical Society of Wisconsin

Boom Times

Nels Wickstrom and family in front of their log home in Florence County, in 1893. *State Historical Society of Wisconsin*

When the Erie Canal opened in 1825, immigrants finally had an all-water route to the Midwest, and adventurous types took advantage of it. Germans were by far the largest group that came to Wisconsin, but English, Irish, Scandinavians, and later Poles also arrived in large numbers. Over the next decades, clusters of immigrants founded communities that bear their stamp to this day, including Danes in Racine, Swiss in New Glarus, Norwegians in Mt. Horeb, Belgians in Kewaunee County, and Icelandic on Washington Island, northeast of the Door Peninsula. Between 1840 and 1850, the state's population jumped from 30,945 to 305,391.

In the southwest corner of the state, where Native Americans had mined and scavenged lead since at least the middle of the 18th century, Cornish miners came by the boatload and by ox-drawn land schooners, many of them squatting on

Indian lands. The purest form of lead ore, galena, drew them to the bustling settlement that came to be known as Mineral Point. By 1840, the area was producing more than half the lead in the country, but by 1845 the ore had run out. Before long farmers supplanted miners, and an economy based on agriculture took hold.

The Peshtigo Fire

On the same day in 1871 that a large part of Chicago burned to the ground, an even more devastating fire destroyed the booming lumber town of Peshtigo, in northern Wisconsin. It remains the deadliest fire in U.S. history. More than 1,200 people died, and more than 1.25 million acres of forest were consumed.

A small Wisconsin town near La Crosse, c. 1890s. *State Historical Society of Wisconsin*

"DOUBTLESS A DAIRYMAN IS A MORE VALUABLE CITIZEN IN THE long run than a prospector or miner, but he does not so easily appeal to the imagination."

Hamlin Garland, A Daughter of the Middle Border, *1922*

"Speak to a cow as you would a lady."

William D. Hoard, 19th-century Wisconsin governor
and "Father of American Dairying"

Say "Cheese"

Jersey cows in Dane County. *Photo Zane Williams*

The dairy agriculture for which Wisconsin is famous was not the first type of farming tried. Wheat was the crop of choice until the 1860s, when farmers who grew it, having exhausted the soil, headed west to Minnesota and the Dakotas. The Scandinavians and Germans who replaced them at first resisted the idea of dairying on a large scale. Most farms kept a cow or two for home use, but the difficulty of transporting perishable milk and butter any distance made bigger markets impossible. The Wisconsin Dairyman's Association, formed in

1872, streamlined the buying and selling process and introduced inspections and quality control. (Previously, some Wisconsin butter had been sold in Chicago as axle grease.)

Even more critical to the success of dairying was the establishment of cheese factories. Cheese traveled better than butter and had the advantage of using whole milk instead of just the butterfat. When farmers learned to coordinate their efforts with those of skilled cheesemakers, profitable new markets were born. The introduction of the silo, enabling year-round cattle feeding (hence, milk production), further transformed dairying in the 1880s. Today dairying accounts for 60% of the state's $6 billion agriculture industry.

Reclining Herd **by Schomer Lichtner, 1962.**
Collection Mark and Sigrid Cullickson,
Milwaukee. Photo Jenny Bohr

Cheesemakers working on a vat of cheese. *Photo Richard Hamilton Smith/Corbis*

Crazy about Curds

Along with waxed cheeses in the shape of cows, plastic bags of unpressed, unaged cheddar cheese curds are a familiar sight in the state's grocery stores and cheese-factory shops. The mild, bite-sized chunks are a popular snack among the lactose tolerant. The freshest curds squeak when bitten into.

Nautical Wisconsin

With hundreds of miles of coastline along Lake Superior and Lake Michigan, Wisconsin has an active maritime tradition of shipping, shipbuilding, and commercial fishing. Superior, with twin city Duluth, Minnesota, has the largest harbor on the Great Lakes and is one of the farthest-inland and deepest freshwater ports in the world. Millions of tons of grain and ore pass through it every year.

The shipyards at Sturgeon Bay. *Below:* Palmer Johnson, located in Sturgeon Bay in Door County, is one of the world's leading builders of yachts today. *Both, Photo Zane Williams*

Along the state's eastern edge, port cities share a colorful past. Sturgeon Bay was an early important shipbuilding center, taking advantage of the nearby tracts of native oak as well

as its pivotal location on the Door Peninsula, with channels connecting Lake Michigan to the Fox and Wisconsin Rivers and, ultimately, the Mississippi. Ships and boats are still built there—from naval minesweepers to tugboats to custom yachts. Although less active now, Kewaunee and Manitowoc both had their day in the sun, with Kewaunee once rivaling Chicago as a maritime center, and Manitowoc home to a flourishing shipbuilding industry. In the 19th century Sheboygan was an important port of entry for immigrants and, halfway between Manitowoc and Milwaukee, a prime spot along the Lake Michigan shipping lane.

Dry Dock by **Edmund Lewandowski, 1998.** *Collection of the West Bend Art Museum*

Overall Satisfaction

Would OshKosh B'Gosh bib overalls be such a fashion icon if they came from Eau Claire? Hard to know. The loose-fitting, many-pocketed pants were first made in Oshkosh in 1895 as rugged wear for farmers and railroad workers, but these days are worn by many who don't know a post-hole digger from a hole in the ground. Children's bib overalls were first offered in 1962; today children's wear accounts for 95% of sales.

The OshKosh logo. *Courtesy OshKosh B'Gosh* **Right:** American Girl dolls—and books— from the Pleasant Company. *Courtesy Pleasant Company*

Girls 'n' Dolls

What do girls want? Molly and her roller skates. Kirsten and her steamer trunk. Former teacher Pleasant T. Rowland founded the Pleasant Company in Middleton in 1986, and the company soon developed a loyal national following for its ethnically sensitive American Girl dolls representing different geographic areas and periods in U.S. history. Acquired by Mattel in 1998, the line of merchandise now includes books, a magazine, and clothes for the human owners of Molly, Kirsten, and their friends.

Think Sink

When John Michael Kohler put an enamel finish on a "horse trough/hog scalder" and called it a bathtub in 1873, his Sheboygan-based iron- and steel-products company suddenly was in the plumbing business. Today, Kohler kitchen and bathroom sinks and plumbing fixtures are internationally known. Company scion Walter J. Kohler served as governor of Wisconsin from 1929 to 1931; his son, Walter Jr., from 1951 to 1957.

A Kohler bathtub.
Courtesy Kohler. Below:
**The Harley-Davidson
2001 FLSTF Fatboy.**
Courtesy Harley-Davidson

H.O.G. Heaven

It seems fitting that Milwaukeeans William Harley and Arthur Davidson were only 21 and 20, respectively, when they first began trying to take the work out of bicycling in 1901. The result of their experiments was to become a quintessential symbol of youth and freedom. Today the Harley-Davidson company remains headquartered in Milwaukee and continues to dominate the U.S. superheavyweight motorcycle market. H.O.G. (Harley Owners' Group) races and festivals all over the world draw thousands of bikers and their admirers every year.

Seeing Milwaukee.

ADAPTED FROM PUCK.

Milwaukee: A Rich Brew

Milwaukee's reputation as a beer-happy town is completely deserved. The city's German roots go deep; by the 1880s, 35% of its population was German born.

While that influence is still strongly felt, today the area is the most ethnically varied in the state. Nearly a third of Milwaukee's residents are African American, and the city is home to large populations of Hispanics and Native Americans as well as people of European descent.

A postcard presents the highlights of a tour of Milwaukee. *State Historical Society of Wisconsin. Right:* German immigrants helped establish a beer industry in Wisconsin with the introduction of hops. *State Historical Society of Wisconsin*

These days Milwaukee manufactures more machinery and electrical equipment than lager or ale. But it will always be Beer City.

In their heyday, three big breweries—Miller, Schlitz, and Pabst—and many smaller ones operated there. Early beermakers were drawn by the plentiful ice and subterranean caves that extended the brewing

season in the days before refrigeration. When Chicago's water supply was damaged in the Great Fire of 1871, Milwaukee came to the rescue with shipments of beer. Prohibition was a difficult time; the day it was repealed, city brewers shipped 15 million bottles of beer. Today, of the Big Three, only Miller remains, although small, specialty brewers (and thousands of enthusiastic beer drinkers) keep the city's proudest tradition alive.

Frederic Miller's original Plank-Road Brewery in Milwaukee, c. 1855. The Miller Brewing Company continues to brew Miller High Life on the same site. *Courtesy Miller Brewing Company.* Left: View looking east along Grand Avenue, the main business street, toward the Milwaukee River, 1925. *Photo Underwood & Underwood/Corbis*

A Ho Chunk powwow in Black River Falls. *Opposite above:* Preparing traps at the winter encampment of Lac du Flambeau. *Opposite below:* "Honor the Earth" powwow in Lac Courte Oreilles. *All, Photo Zane Williams Below:* This sewing basket was made by Ho Chunk artist Ruth Cloud of Baraboo, c. 1986. *State Historical Society of Wisconsin*

The Native American population of Wisconsin these days numbers upward of 40,000 people. Most live on the Ojibwe (Chippewa), Stockbridge-Munsee, Potawatomi, Sakaogon, Menominee, Lac Courte Oreilles, and Oneida reservations in the northern part of the state; Ho Chunk (Winnebago) are a non-reservation group. The Menominee are the state's oldest residents; the heavily forested county of Menominee is their reservation. The Oneida, part of the Iroquois Confederacy, arrived in the early 1800s, displaced from New York.

At the reservation at Lac du Flambeau

(named by French explorers for the Ojibwe practice of spearfishing from canoes at night by torchlight), Ojibwe traditions are very much alive. Waswagoning, an authentic re-creation of a native village on Moving Cloud Lake, offers demonstrations of tanning, canoe building, maple syruping, dancing,

and weaving in birchbark lodges. In the town of Lac du Flambeau, the Ojibwe Museum and Cultural Center displays centuries-old artifacts and modern examples of Ojibwe quilling and other crafts.

Bascom Hall, the main administration building, was built in 1859. *Below and opposite:* Memorial Union Terrace sits on the shore of Lake Mendota, a prime spot for sailing. The Memorial Union is the center of student life and includes the Rathskeller, a popular place to grab a bite to eat and hang out. *All, Photo Zane Williams*

Idea Factory

The University of Wisconsin-Madison's tradition of against-the-grain thinking goes back to its founding in 1849. The school's early leaders had a strong sense of obligation to residents in all parts of the state; their "Wisconsin Idea" led to educational, health, and agricultural extension services far from the Madison campus. Today, 40,000 students—40 percent of

them outside the "traditional student" 18-to-22 age bracket—attend the school, where social activism and a free exchange of ideas continue to flourish. Alone among American universities, UW-M is home to two daily student newspapers, the *Cardinal* and the *Badger Herald,* with unabashedly opposing points of view. Since 1990 the university has produced more volunteers for the Peace Corps than any other school.

Achievements in many fields have won acclaim for university researchers. UW-M innovations include the first reliable method for measuring butterfat content in milk, easy-to-swallow pill coatings, iodized salt, artificial snow, "perfect" pizza cheese, the National Organization for Women, and the Dictionary of American Regional English.

"WHATEVER MAY BE THE LIMITATIONS WHICH TRAMMEL INQUIRY elsewhere, we believe the great State University of Wisconsin should ever encourage that continual and fearless sifting and winnowing by which alone the truth can be found."

From an 1894 board of regents report exonerating
economics professor Richard T. Ely of charges that he taught pernicious ideas

Beauty and the Barn

The red or white wood-frame dairy barn is perhaps the most enduring—and photogenic—form of vernacular architecture in Wisconsin. Family dairy farming is on the wane, but many well-maintained, 100-year-old barns are still in use. Two-story "bank" barns housed cattle on the first floor and stored hay or grain on the second. Older barns' first-floor walls were built with fieldstone or quarried rock; some of the oldest have half-timber walls, with brick filling in the spaces between the heavy oak supports. Concrete walls usually mean post-1920 construction.

Rooflines vary, and sometimes give clues to the barn's ethnic origins. Simple gable roofs were

Farm and cornfields in Iowa County. *Right:* A gambrel-roofed red barn in Rock County. A "gambrel" is the bent part of an animal's back leg. *Both, Photo Zane Williams*

Bank barns with gambrel roofs are found in all parts of the state. They are so called because they were built against a bank or hill for easier access to the upper-level threshing area. *Photo Zane Williams. Below:* The 1998 U.S. postage stamp celebrating the sesquicentennial of the state of Wisconsin featured a photograph by prolific native son Zane Williams.

used on early log barns, English, Norwegian, and some Finnish barns, as well as on smaller farm buildings and houses. Four-planed gambrel roofs, sometimes with dormers or other variations, are the most common type in Wisconsin; they offer more storage space under their eaves than the gabled kind. Round or arched roofs, their curves descending almost to the ground, became popular beginning in the 1940s.

The University of Wisconsin–Extension, the Wisconsin Trust for Historic Preservation, and the State Historical Society

Dewy Morning by
Adolph Robert Shulz,
n.d. *Courtesy Wright
Museum of Art, Beloit
College*

of Wisconsin have joined forces to try to save the most significant of Wisconsin's old agricultural buildings. One result of their efforts is the Barns Network of Wisconsin (Barns N.O.W.), a not-for-profit organization dedicated to the appreciation and preservation of the state's historic barns. Participants in its Adopt-a-Barn program help to restore barns that have fallen into disrepair in exchange for using the refurbished buildings for dances and other community events.

Girls' Band Playing to Cows at University of Wisconsin Dairy Barn by Angus McVicar, 1930. *State Historical Society of Wisconsin, McVicar Collection. Below:* Barn raising at the turn of the 20th century was a communal affair. *State Historical Society of Wisconsin*

"WHAT DID THAT FEEL LIKE WHEN YOU WENT INTO A BARN ON A WINDY DAY . . . WHEN THE wind was blowing around the corners and rustling under the eaves, when the pigeons were cooing up on the hayfork track? It was like being in the middle of an orchestra."

Jerry Apps, author of Barns of Wisconsin, *in an interview for Wisconsin Public Television*

The Republican Party was born in a little white schoolhouse in Ripon, in 1854. *Wisconsin Natural Resources Department. Below: Progressive Party Rally by John Steuart Curry, 1938. Madison Art Center*

An Independent Tradition

Wisconsin's tradition of independent politics goes way back. The Republican Party, formed around an antislavery ideology, was born in Ripon in 1854. Robert M. LaFollette, Sr., a progressive Republican who championed child-labor laws and other reforms, was elected to the U.S. House of Representatives in 1885; he later served as governor and senator. In Milwaukee, socialist theories found many adherents late in the century. Victor Berger, an Austrian Jew by birth, and his Social Democrat Party were a force in city politics for decades, and Berger was eventually elected to the U.S. Congress. In 1919,

Sen. Joseph McCarthy tries out an oversize broom sent to him from Little Chute, Wisconsin, to help him "clean up the Capitol," in January 1952. *Corbis.* Below: After anti–Vietnam War student protests escalated at the University of Wisconsin–Madison, the National Guard was called in on February 13, 1969. Here Guards enter the education building. *AP/Wide World Photos*

Wisconsin became the first state to ratify the 19th amendment to the Constitution, granting women the right to vote.

Histrionic Senator Joe McCarthy tapped into the national paranoia about Communism in the early 1950s, hurling accusations against his peers, his enemies, the secretary of state, and many others. Noisy iconoclasm took a different form in the late 1960s and early '70s, when organized protests at the University of Wisconsin–Madison challenging the U.S. role in the war in Vietnam became the model for mobilizing students at other colleges and universities.

Frank Lloyd Wright at his home near Madison. He grew up in the valley across the river. *Photo Thomas Hollyman/Photo Researchers. Below: Taliesin, in Spring Green. Photo P. Guerrero/Taliesin Preservation*

Born in Richland Center in 1867, Frank Lloyd Wright, father of the Prairie School of architecture, remained connected to Wisconsin throughout his life. Before signing on as a draftsman in the Chicago firm of Adler and Sullivan in 1887, he studied civil engineering at the University of Wisconsin in Madison. As a child he enjoyed visiting relatives' farms near Spring Green; he later chose a spot south of the town for a country home he called Taliesin, Welsh for "shining brow." The bucolic retreat was the scene of tragedy in 1914,

when seven people, including Mamah Borthwick Cheney, Wright's lover, were murdered there by a servant, who also set a fire that destroyed much of the house. In 1932 Wright founded the Taliesin Fellowship at the rebuilt site and worked with apprentices on important projects there.

"NO HOUSE SHOULD EVER BE ON ANY HILL OR ON anything. It should be of the hill, belonging to it."

Frank Lloyd Wright on Taliesin,
from An Autobiography, *1932*

Wright Sites

About 45 Wright structures (including those at Taliesin) were built in Wisconsin. Some of the most important are:

A. D. German Warehouse, Richland Center, 1915

S. C. Johnson (Johnson Wax) Administration Building and Research Tower, Racine, 1936 and 1944

"Wingspread" (Herbert F. Johnson House), Wind Point, 1937

Unitarian Church (Meeting House), Shorewood Hills, 1947

Annunciation Greek Orthodox Church, Wauwatosa, 1956

Dewey Wright House, Wausau, 1956

The Unitarian Meeting House in Shorewood Hills.

Monona Terrace, viewed from Lake Monona. *Photo Zane Williams. Above:* The view from the living room of Taliesin. *Photo Farrell Grehan/Corbis*

Cheddar and Beer Soup

2 sticks butter
½ cup finely chopped onion
½ cup finely chopped celery
1½ cups flour
2 quarts beef broth
2 cups milk
1 cup beer (flat)
2 tsp. liquid smoke
1 tsp. hot red pepper sauce
3 tblsp. Worcestershire sauce
3 cups shredded cheddar
   cheese
½ cup finely chopped parsley

Sauté onion and celery in the butter until soft. Add flour; stir over
medium heat about 5 minutes.
Slowly add broth, then milk, stir-
ring constantly. Add beer, liquid
smoke, hot red pepper sauce and
Worcestershire sauce. Bring just
to boil. Remove from heat. Add
cheese; stir until melted. Return
to low heat; do not let soup boil.
Stir in parsley; adjust seasonings.
Serves 10.
From the Dairy Council of Wisconsin

A fish boil in Fish Creek.
Photo Zane Williams

The Wisconsin Table

Wisconsin is a meat-and-potatoes state, with all
the variations you would expect and some you
wouldn't. In Milwaukee, look for sauerbraten
and German potato salad as well as sausages and
"butter burgers"—hamburgers fried in butter. In
the southwest, around Mineral Point and Shullsburg, restaurants serve Cornish pasties, a meat
pie originally made as a meal miners could take
to work.

Door County is famous for the fish boil, a
melange of steaming whitefish, potatoes, and
onions served with cole slaw and dark bread. This
is also cherry territory, and many local specialties
feature the fruit. Norwegian-American grocers
around Stoughton and Mt. Horeb can supply you
with lefse (like potato tortillas) and gjetost (goat

cheese), as well as lingonberries and lutefisk. Racine bakeries sell kringle, a pastry introduced by Danish immigrants. And throughout the state, frozen custard provides an extra-rich, eggy alternative to ice cream.

A 1906 advertisement for Pabst Blue Ribbon. *American Heritage Collection. Left:* Brats and other sausages at the Village Market in Waunakee. *Photo Zane Williams. Above:* University of Wisconsin students pause for a glass of beer at a barn dance in the 1920s. *University of Wisconsin Archives*

Gardens of Earthly Delight

Wisconsinites' talent for growing things is showcased in a number of formal gardens. In Janesville, the Rotary Garden features 13 internationally themed sections, including an English Cottage garden and a French plot given over to flowers used in perfumes. In Hales Corners, near Milwaukee, the Boerner Botanical Gardens has 40 acres of flower gardens, an arboretum, and the largest flowering crabapple orchard in the country. Madison's Olbrich Botanical Gardens, the brainchild of civic-minded attorney Michael Balthazar Olbrich, draws thousands of visitors every year with their acres of roses,

Curtis Prairie, part of the University of Wisconsin Arboretum, is considered the world's oldest prairie and consists of 60 acres of deep-soil tallgrass prairie. In early fall, Indian grass and 10-foot-tall big bluestem grass flourish. *Photo Zane Williams. Below:* The Peony Garden at the Boerner Botanical Gardens in Hales Corners. *Photo Michael Shedlock/New England Stock Photo*

wildflowers, specialty gardens, and tropical forest conservatory.

Also in Madison is the University of Wisconsin Arboretum, considered a pioneer in restoring and managing ecological communities. Seventy years ago, most of the land included in its current acreage was cultivated fields and pastures that had fallen into disuse. Today the 1,240-acre arboretum is a research and teaching facility specializing in the reestablishment of historic landscapes. The site includes wetlands, forests, and the world's oldest restored tallgrass prairie.

When Ole Evinrude had trouble rowboating ice cream to a picnic site on a hot day in Waukesha County in 1909, he went home and designed a "detachable rowboat motor." In 1924, Vilas County's Carl Eliason added skis, a tractor tread, and a small engine to a toboggan and came up with a primitive snowmobile. He patented an improved design in 1927.

The Great Outdoors

It's not only tourists who take advantage of Wisconsin's natural recreational facilities. No resident lives more than a

short drive from one of the state's thousands of lakes. Especially in the north, hunting and fishing have long defined the culture; it's a poor excuse for a supper club that doesn't have venison or locally caught fish on its menu. Lovers of the outdoors come motorized and nonmotorized. The state has more than 900 miles of all-terrain vehicle

(ATV) trails, a number of which run along abandoned railroad grades. But that's nothing compared to the 22,000 miles of snowmobile trails, many marked and groomed by local snowmobiling clubs.

The non-motorized prefer canoeing or rafting on some rollicking river; opportunities also abound for hiking and skiing. With its topography of gentle hills occasionally interrupted by steep slopes and flat patches, Wisconsin seems to have been custom sculpted for cross-country skiing. Hundreds of facilities cater to the sport's aficionados, both the classic "track" skiers and fans of flashier, free-style skiing.

Opposite: Ice Fishing, Lake Mendota, by Aaron Bohrod, 1949. Milwaukee Art Museum. ©Estate of Aaron Bohrod/ Licensed by VAGA, N.Y. Opposite bottom: Professional snowmobile racer. Photo Richard Hamilton Smith/Corbis. Below: Flyfishing in Door County. Photo Zane Williams

Rockin'

Devil's Lake State Park, the state's only designated rock-climbing park, draws more visitors annually than Yellowstone with its billion-and-a-half-year-old quartzite bluffs and spookily deep lake. The dramatic landscape just south of Baraboo is a result of glacial action 10,000 to 70,000 years ago, when millions of tons of melting ice and rocky debris pushed the ancient Wisconsin River into its current configuration.

Rock climbing in Devil's Lake State Park. *Both, Photo Zane Williams*

Gangster Retreats

Law-abiding citizens aren't the only ones who find Wisconsin a good place to get away from it all. In the 1920s, the town of Couderay, near Hayward, was the site of a retreat used by Al Capone, who liked to fish. He had a fieldstone lodge built with 18-inch bulletproof walls in the middle of 400 acres of grounds, along with a machine-gun turret and a bunkhouse. A lake provided landing space for planes bringing in bootleg liquor from Canada. These days Capone's eight-car garage is a supper club called The Hideout.

Bank robber John Dillinger also favored Wisconsin when he wanted to cool off after a big job or jail break, and once used a Spider Lake resort called Little Bohemia for this purpose.

The Dells

So, what's a dell? No, it's not the kind the farmer is in. The word comes from *dalles,* the name given by French explorers to a spectacular seven-mile stretch of the Wisconsin River. Native American legend says the dramatically twisty gorge was created by a giant serpent. Geologists say it was formed when melting glaciers sent torrents of water down the riverbed. Whatever their origins, the water-carved sandstone formations along the river reveal nature at its most artful. Tourists have always thought so; by the mid-1850s the Dells was a resort area.

Native Americans were hired to jump back and forth at Stand Rock to amuse tourists, until one man fell to his death. Today, a dog fulfills the same duty. *Photo H. H. Bennett. Courtesy George Eastman House Collection Right:* Amusement parks, motels, and restaurants line the main strip in the town of Wisconsin Dells. *Photo Zane Williams*

A tour boat plies the waters of the Lower Wisconsin Dells. *Photo Zane Williams. Below:* Photographer Henry Hamilton Bennett set up shop in the Dells in 1875. His pictures helped turn the Dells into a tourist mecca. *Photo H. H. Bennett*

Natural beauty still exists at the Dells but one must wade through kitsch to find it. The popular tourist destination has a mind-boggling array of restaurants, motels, shops, themed amusements, water parks, children's activities, and tour operations. Long-standing attractions include rides on the "ducks," refurbished amphibious vehicles from World War II. And of course there are the thrill-a-minute enterprises of Dells entrepreneur Tommy Bartlett, whose air-and-water show and Robot World have drawn crowds (and handed out bumper stickers) for decades.

In 14-below-zero weather, the Green Bay Packer faithful cheer on their team at a championship game. *Corbis Below:* Packers quarterback Brett Favre signals a touchdown after completing a pass. *Photo Joe Picciolo/AFP/Corbis*

The Big Leagues

It's impossible not to like the Green Bay Packers. They're one of the original National Football League franchises. They're

from the smallest city with an NFL team and are owned—not for profit—by its residents. They play uncomplainingly in the coldest, snowiest weather. They inspire diehard fans to wear wedges of foam-rubber cheese on their heads. They have won 12 championships, including Super Bowls I, II, and XXX. And they came to prominence under the quotable Vince Lombardi, who had a thing about winning. Now that's a football team.

But there are other professional sports here. In Milwaukee, baseball's Brewers have a following, though many fans still have not gotten over Hammerin' Hank Aaron and their beloved Braves' jilting them for Atlanta in 1966. The Brewers came to town in 1970; in 1997, the team moved from the American League to the National League, where it watches as Atlanta dominates. Basketball's Bucks also have passionate fans, some of whom look back on the early 1970s as the team's glory years. In 1971 center Lew Alcindor (later Kareem Abdul-Jabbar) and guard Oscar Robertson led the Bucks to their only NBA title. Known for tough, hard-nosed play, the team has rebounded recently, making it into the playoffs in 1999 and 2000.

"I HAVE NO PATIENCE WITH THE SMALL HURTS THAT ARE bothering most of you."

Vince Lombardi to his players, 1959

Vince Lombardi became coach of the struggling Packers in 1958; in 1961, the team won the NFL championship. The Packers went on to win the first two Super Bowls, in 1967 and 1968. *Poster Courtesy Spencer Walts. Left:* Hank Aaron crosses the plate after hitting a three-run homer in the 1957 World Series featuring the Braves and the New York Yankees. In 1966, the Braves moved to Atlanta. *Bettmann/Corbis*

A stunt pilot performs in Oshkosh. *Below:* One of the many unique planes to be found at the Fly-In. *Both, Photo Zane Williams*

Flying High in Oshkosh

Site of the Experimental Aircraft Association's annual, week-long AirVenture, a.k.a the Fly-In, Oshkosh is transformed every summer into a colorful gathering place for pilots and plane lovers from all over the country. A big part of the attraction is the chance to examine, close up, hundreds of home-built, antique, eccentric, and classic aircraft, including military planes, ultralights, and rotorcraft, and talk to other aviation fans. Many of the planes see action in the daily air show, with stunt pilots providing sky-high entertainment. Oshkosh is the year-round home of the EAA's Air Adventure Museum.

At Road America, Elkhart Lake's international speedway, Indy-style cars, U.S. Grand Prix motorcycles, vintage vehicles and other supercharged wheels race on the longest natural road-racing course in the U.S.

Ladies and Gentlemen . . .

Circus history is alive and well in Wisconsin. In the last decades of the 19th century, 28 different circuses, including P. T. Barnum's first, wintered in Delavan, where a statue of a rearing elephant stands in the town square. In Baraboo, hometown of the seven Ringling brothers and once the winter quarters of the Ringling Brothers Circus, the Circus World Museum's collection of rebuilt circus wagons, posters, photos, and other memorabilia provides a glimpse of life under the big top. For the annual Great Circus Parade in Milwaukee each July, the wagons are transported to town by steam train and roll through the streets just as they did in the good old days.

The Ringling brothers hailed from Baraboo, now home to the Circus World Museum. The museum's collection includes memorabilia such as this 1894 poster. *Courtesy Circus World Museum. Left:* A tiger in a wagon for the Great Circus Parade in Milwaukee. *Photo Zane Williams*

Hamlin Garland with friend. *Culver Pictures. Below: Zona Gale. Culver Pictures*

Word People

Wisconsin writers often show a strong affinity for nature. Hamlin Garland won a Pulitzer Prize in 1922 for *A Daughter of the Middle Border,* which, like his earlier *A Son of the Middle Border,* told of life in rural Wisonsin in the state's formative years. Reporter and literary editor Sterling North chronicled the exploits of his pet raccoon in *Rascal,* which was made into a Disney film. Celebrated children's novelist Marguerite Henry wrote about horses; several of her books were also filmed. Poet Lorine Niedecker focused on the area around her birthplace, marshy Blackhawk Island, near Ft. Atkinson.

Playwright and novelist Zona Gale, whose play *Miss Lulu Bett* won a Pulitzer Prize in 1921, took a different tack; her

works reflected her interest in politics and social reform. Novelist and short-story writer Edna Ferber (*Show Boat, So Big, Giant*) began her writing career as a teenage reporter in Appleton; she later wrote for the *Milwaukee Journal.* Probably the state's most prolific writer, August Derleth published more than 150 books on a wide range of subjects, from historical novels and poems to tales of the macabre.

"THE HOUSE IS STILL THERE, ITS STONE WALLS AGED IN THE SUNLIGHT of the years, yellowed where it stands on top of the highest of the moraine hills across the blue Wisconsin, east of Sac Prairie."
August Derleth, The House of Moonlight, *1953. Sauk Prairie—the actual spelling—is comprised of the towns Prairie du Sac and Sauk City.*

Laura Ingalls Wilder brought her Wisconsin childhood to life for children everywhere. *Courtesy Laura Ingalls Wilder Home Association* *Below:* A reconstructed log cabin, built on the site of Wilder's birthplace. *Photo Oliver Grotthus*

Laura Ingalls Wilder

Laura Elizabeth Ingalls was born a few miles north of Pepin, a tiny town on the Mississippi River, in 1867. Her childhood was spent on the move—to Missouri, Kansas, back to Wisconsin, Minnesota, Iowa, the Dakota Territory— as her father tried farming and other professions. She met and married Almanzo Wilder in her teens, while working as a teacher. In her 60s, with the help of her daughter Rose, she began writing down stories she had told her children. The first, *Little House in the Big Woods,* was based on memories of her early life in Wisconsin; it led to seven other *Little House* books, one of the most popular series of children's books ever published.

All of the photographs in *Wisconsin Death Trip* were taken by Charles Von Schaick, a town photographer in Black River Falls; the Von Schaick Collection now belongs to the State Historical Society of Wisconsin. As Lesy writes in his introduction, the pictures "are artful only in so far as he obeyed the most prosaic conventions of portraiture." Yet the photographs have a beautiful eeriness. *Courtesy State Historical Society of Wisconsin*

"Another suicide occurred in this city Sunday afternoon last. . . ."

Michael Lesy's bleak 1973 cult classic *Wisconsin Death Trip* presents photos and newspaper excerpts from the 1890s, when an economic depression triggered an unusually high rate of murder, suicide, contagious disease, business failure, mental illness, and addiction in the town of Black River Falls.

On the Air

Since 1985 radio listeners across the country have been tuning in to an original brand of Wisconsin-inflected humor on Michael Feldman's two-hour Saturday morning show, *Whad'Ya Know?* Broadcast live (syndicated by Public Radio International) from the University of Wisconsin-Madison, the program is both sharp and down-home, combining Feldman's topical monologues, interviews, call-ins, and quizzes with audience participation. The quick-thinking Feldman, a Milwaukee native and former high-school English teacher, has been variously described as a Midwestern Groucho Marx and "the king of small-talk radio."

"JUST BECAUSE MY SHOW IS about nothing doesn't mean that I'm doing it on purpose. I'm trying to be significant; I'm just failing."

Michael Feldman, interviewed for online magazine Fade to Black

On the Tube

Milwaukee was the setting for two popular TV sitcoms that ran in the late 1970s and early '80s but drew on nostalgia for the '50s. *Happy Days* recounted the exploits of Richie Cunningham (Ron Howard), his high-school friends (including the Fonz, a dropout played by Henry Winkler), and family. *Laverne and Shirley,* a *Happy Days* spin-off, made more of the Milwaukee milieu. Its protagonists, the up-for-anything Laverne DeFazio (Penny Marshall) and her cheerfully naive roommate Shirley Feeney (Cindy Williams), juggled their love lives, which often involved bowling dates, with jobs at the fictitious Shotz Brewery.

The Fonz, Richie, and Potsie (Anson Williams) hang out 1950s style in *Happy Days. Photofest. Left: Laverne and Shirley* first aired in 1976. A show about two bottle-cappers making their dreams come true in Milwaukee became the top-rated sitcom in the country in its second season. *Photofest. Opposite:* Michael Feldman in his studio. *Photo Zane Williams*

On Stage

The American Players Theatre in Spring Green presents open-air performances of classic plays, as in this 2000 production of *A Midsummer Night's Dream*. Photo Zane Williams

One of the brightest lights on the Wisconsin theater scene is the American Players Theatre in Spring Green. Since 1979 the company has been offering Shakespearean productions and classic plays in an outdoor setting; audiences sit on cushioned seats in a natural, hillside amphitheater. The Peninsula Players, who operate just north of Fish Creek on the Door Peninsula, may be the country's oldest summer theater. They've been putting on Broadway plays and musicals in the open air for more than 60 years.

Milwaukee is home to more than a dozen theater companies, including adventurous Theatre X, which produces

Ten Chimneys

This 60-acre estate in Waukesha County was once the summer home of actors Alfred Lunt (who was born in Milwaukee) and Lynn Fontanne. From the mid-1920s through the 1960s, the Lunts entertained and worked on projects there with leading theater artists, including Helen Hayes, Katharine Hepburn, Laurence Olivier, and Noel Coward. The Ten Chimneys Foundation is working to preserve the estate, which it hopes to re-establish as a museum and center for theater and arts education.

original work generated by the company and showcases young performers in an experimental late-night series. Started in 1969, Theatre X counts actor Willem Dafoe among its alumni. The Milwaukee Chamber Theatre, in the city's historic Third Ward, specializes in classic and contemporary plays with a literary flavor. Its well-attended Shaw Festival is an annual event. In Madison, the Madison Repertory Theatre is known for its productions of modern and classic stage works. More experimental fare is regularly offered by Broom Street Theater and the Mercury Players Theater Company.

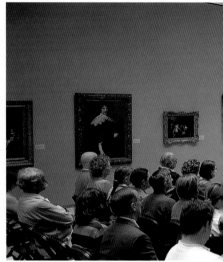

The Milwaukee Symphony Orchestra tours statewide, nationally, and internationally.
Photo Zane Williams

The well-regarded Milwaukee Symphony Orchestra, under music director Andreas Delfs, plays a full season of concerts in Milwaukee, tours all over the state (as well as nationally and internationally), runs educational programs for children, records extensively, and reaches more than 200 markets through radio broadcasts. Itzhak Perlman, Nadja Salerno-Sonnenberg, Emanuel Ax, and other major artists have soloed with the orchestra.

The Pro Arte Quartet has been in residence at the University of Wisconsin–Madison since 1940, when the internationally prominent string ensemble, then touring the U.S., was stranded by the outbreak of World War II. The group was founded in Belgium in 1912. The quartet continues to present premieres of new works, many written especially for the ensemble. 🐄

Chamber music at the Elvehjem Museum of Art, University of Wisconsin. *Photo Zane Williams*

Pas de Deux

Established in 1970, the Milwaukee Ballet is known for its popular annual production of *The Nutcracker* and also for its ventures into less classical dance domains. Works in its repertoire have touched on subjects including AIDS, Native American traditions, the power of women, and the paintings of Henri Rousseau. Other audience favorites have featured jitterbugging to the music of Glenn Miller in "Harvest Moon" and the patriotic march rhythms of "Stars and Stripes."

Milwaukee Ballet dancers Alyce Andrews and Lee-Wei Chao perform Igal Perry's *Eye of the Storm*. Photo Tim Evans/Milwaukee Ballet

Couples face the music and dance at a polka festival in Wisconsin Dells. *Photo Zane Williams. Below:* An 1844 engraving of "La Polka." *American Heritage Collection*

Polka Fever

Designated the state dance in 1993, polka's roots in Wisconsin go back to the 19th-century influx of Eastern and Central European immigrants. Today polka music is unavoidable at wedding receptions and always within easy reach on AM radio. The bouncy, mood-altering peasant dance in 2/4 time, derived from Bohemian folk dancing in the early 19th century, was customized by many different European cultures, including Polish, Czech, Dutch, and Swiss. The Wisconsin version incorporates those and other styles. Kenosha and New Glarus are among the many towns that host annual polka festivals.

View of the Fox River by Henry Vianden, 1885–88. *Milwaukee Art Museum*

Most of Wisconsin's early landscapists were academically trained European immigrants. Prominent among them was Henry Vianden, an engraver and painter from Germany, who settled in Milwaukee in 1849 and became an influential teacher, even as he continued to paint precisely rendered outdoor scenes. Bernhard Schneider and Richard Lorenz, two other 19th-century artists captivated by the natural world, often painted rural areas and small towns. Of later artists who looked to nature for inspira-

tion, Robert von Neumann, Schomer Lichtner, Ruth Grotenrath, and noted regionalist John Steuart Curry stand out. Curry, whose murals are on view in many public buildings, became artist-in-residence at the University of Wisconsin–Madison in 1936.

An early Wisconsin sculptor, Vinnie Reem-Hoxie, was the first woman and the youngest artist ever chosen to do an important sculpture for the United States Senate. Her posthumous life-size portrait of Abraham Lincoln stands in the National Capital Rotunda.

Two years after the death of John Steuart Curry in 1946, Aaron Bohrod, a Chicago-born watercolorist and oil

Main Street, Alma by
Gustave Moeller, 1925.
Milwaukee Art Museum

By far the most
famous painter born in
Wisconsin, Georgia
O'Keeffe grew up on a
farm in Sun Prairie, a
few miles northwest of
Madison, where she
received art lessons at
home and encourage-
ment at school. She
left for Chicago in 1905,
at age 17, her mind
made up to be an
artist. A contemporary
of hers, Mark Tobey,
was born in Center-
ville; he went on to
achieve international
renown as a master
abstract expressionist.

painter, was named his replacement as artist-in-residence
at the University of Wisconsin–Madison. Although
known for "magic realism" and trompe l'oeil still lifes,
Bohrod was sensitive to place, and often sketched Wisconsin barns, swamps, and small towns. Another important Wisconsin artist is Milwaukee-born John Wilde,
whose dreamy, allegorical paintings often combine
elements from the natural world with nude figures in
surprising contexts.

Autumn Field by Mark Tobey, 1957. © ARS, NY. Courtesy National Museum of American Art, Smithsonian Institution, Washington, D.C./Art Resource, NY. Below: Happy, Crazy American Animals and a Man and Lady at My Place by John Wilde, 1961. Wilde was born in Milwaukee and taught at the University of Wisconsin–Madison from 1948 to 1982. Courtesy National Museum of American Art, Smithsonian Institution, Washington, D.C./Art Resource

Wisconsin has long been a place where the eccentric, unschooled, visionary, and intuitive could pursue their art in peace, often on a big scale. And often outdoors. Made with materials commonly found around the house, barn, or garage, their artwork is often years in the making. Their pure expressiveness knows no bounds.

Wisconsin Concrete Park

When Fred Smith started building large concrete sculptures studded with rocks, beer bottles, and glass insulator knobs on his property south of Phillips in 1948, his neighbors didn't know what to think. Sixteen years later, they still weren't sure. Smith, a former lumberjack who could neither read nor write and was in his 60s when he began the project, eventually completed more than 250 statues representing friends, characters from folklore, soldiers, pioneers, horses, kings, queens, angels, lions, and fish.

Grandview

Concrete embellished with marbles, broken china, and seashells is a Wisconsin specialty. In 1937, another self-taught artist, Austro-Hungarian immigrant Nicholas Engelbert, started using those materials to create more than 40 large figures on his farm, Grandview, outside Hollandale. A tribute to his new life in America, the statues depict Paul Bunyan, Uncle Sam, Snow White and the Seven Dwarfs, and many different animals. He also made paintings in which he depicted his sculpture park.

La Reau's World of Miniature

Clarice and Paul La Reau used Styrofoam to create the World of Miniature outside their one-story brick home in Pardeeville. They have completed small, precise replicas of the Capitol Building in Washington (1,487 hours to construct), the Statue of Liberty, the United Nations building, *Gone With the Wind*'s Tara, the Great Wall of China, Egyptian pyramids, Stonehenge, a Kentucky Fried Chicken outlet, and many other structures.

Forevertron

Five miles south of Baraboo lies the world's largest sculpture. It was constructed by scrap artisan Tom Every, better known as Dr. Evermor, out of 320 tons of old carburetors and other gizmos acquired through his salvage and dismantling business. The *Forevertron*, a bristling sci-fi megacontraption that stands as a monument to 19th-century inventiveness and time-travel fantasies, dominates a landscape crowded with mechanical creatures, including a 70-member Bird Band.

Dickeyville Grotto

Built by Father Mathias Wernerus between 1925 and 1931, the Holy Ghost Park celebrates religion and patriotism. The grotto's massive concrete altars, shrines, fountains, arches, and statuary nooks are encrusted with a dizzying array of materials, including rocks, shells, fossils, Indian relics, costume jewelry, hornets' nests, fragments of glass, and dishware. The park surrounds Holy Ghost Catholic Church in Dickeyville.

Museum of Woodcarving

Just north of Shell Lake, the Museum of Woodcarving displays 100 life-size carvings and 400 smaller pieces—all on biblical themes—by wood sculptor Joseph T. Barta, who died in 1972. Inspired by a series of dreams and divine revelations, the rough-hewn pieces include Adam and Eve's banishment from the Garden of Eden, Daniel in the lions' den, and an enormous Last Supper, four and a half years in the making.

Glass Church

Paul and Matilda Wegner's Glass Church and prayer garden are a glittery surprise to many visitors in Monroe County. Begun as a retirement project in the 1930s, the sculptures in reinforced concrete, inlaid with glass and china, commemorate the life the Wegners enjoyed in the U.S. following their emigration from Germany. Pieces include a ship, a harp, a steamship, and an anniversary cake. The front of the Glass Church features Lutheran and Catholic imagery and a Star of David over the door, with the inscription "One God, One Brotherhood."

Phantom Buck II **by Charles Munch, 2000. Munch lives in Bear Valley.** *Courtesy Wisconsin Academy Gallery*

Adventurous artists in many media work all over the state. Pieces by them are included in the collections of the Madison Art Center and the Milwaukee Art Museum, and in independent galleries in both cities. Milwaukee is home to a number of art dealers who specialize in the work of contemporary and emerging artists. Some of the best new work may be found at galleries on the east side of the city and in the Third Ward district and environs; Adambomb Gallerie and One Nation Gallery are two likely spots. Another is the Frederick Layton Gallery at the Milwaukee Institute of Art and Design. 🐄

Carved and Mosaic Sculptures by Mary Nohl, 1960–1980. Nohl's sculptures echo the rougher mosaics of Wisconsin's large-scale Outsider art. *J. M. Kohler Art Center. Below: Nin Minwendamia* by Tom Uttech,1999. Uttech's romantic paintings portray the wilderness of northern Wisconsin. The artist resides in Saukville. *Courtesy Wisconsin Academy Gallery*

Full House

Ever had a dream in which you staggered claustrophobically through an endless maze of rooms and hallways crammed with dolls, chandeliers, carousel animals, theater organs, and Santa Clauses while mechanical music played in the background? Maybe it was no dream; maybe you visited the House on the Rock, near Spring Green. It was built

in the 1940s by would-be architect Alex Jordan, who meant to parody Frank Lloyd Wright. Jordan's obsessive collection of antiques and curiosities has been open to the public since 1961.

Nothing to Fear

If it's real, the hodag lives in Rhinelander. If it's not, it still lives in Rhinelander. Northern Wisconsin's own, highly local mythical beast, the hodag, was first "sighted" in 1896, when a local man produced a photo purporting to show a wild beast that had leaped out at him in the woods. Seven feet long, half lion, half reptile, the horned, clawed creature had a spiky, Triceratops-like spine. The tale was soon revealed as a hoax but the hodag endures in Rhinelander in business names, on T-shirts, and as the high school mascot.

Crack Lumberjacks

You can have your World Wrestling Federation. For a real show of brawn and finesse, nothing beats the annual Lumberjack World Championships in Hayward. Events include the standing chop, underhand chop, springboard chop, double bucking, Jack and Jill sawing, speed climbing and tree topping, log rolling, and other feats of skill and daring.

Winged Victory

The International Crane Foundation in Baraboo is home to the world's most complete collection of crane species, all either threatened or endangered. It is dedicated to protecting and preserving the graceful birds and their wetland habitats. Every spring the foundation sponsors a volunteer count of sandhill cranes, a species found by the thousands along the Mississippi Flyway.

Moo-na Lisa

The ever-enigmatic Mona Lisa—in a Bucky Badger T-shirt—graces a barn 4½ miles west of the town of Gilman on highway 64, in Taylor County. A number of barns were painted with murals as part of the Dairyland Graphics program in the 1970s; others, including this Mona Lisa, were independent productions.

America's Ginsengland

About 95% of all ginseng produced in the United States, much of it destined for export to Hong Kong, is grown in Wisconsin. The bifurcated root, popular as an aphrodisiac and memory sharpener, is a tricky crop. It has been grown in the state, chiefly in the Wausau area, for almost 100 years, ever since four Wisconsin brothers figured out how to cultivate the precious root in artificially shaded raised beds.

Great People

A selective listing of native Wisconsinites, concentrating on the arts.

Gene Wilder (b. 1935), actor; Milwaukee

Don Ameche (1908–1993), actor (*Trading Places, Cocoon*); Kenosha

Lynda Barry (b. 1956), cartoonist, novelist; Richland Center

Willem Dafoe (b. 1955), actor (*The Last Temptation of Christ, Platoon*); Appleton

Tyne Daly (b. 1946), *Cagney and Lacey* actress; Madison

Chris Farley (1964–1997), *Saturday Night Live* actor; Madison

King Camp Gillette (1855–1932), inventor of disposable razor; Fond du Lac

Bobby Hatfield (b. 1940), Righteous Brother; Beaver Dam

Eric Heiden (b. 1958), Olympic gold medalist speed skater; Madison

Woody Herman (1913–1987), clarinetist, saxophone player, bandleader; Milwaukee

Lewis Hine (1874–1940), social-reformist photographer; Oshkosh

Al Jarreau (b. 1940), jazz singer; Milwaukee

Frank King (1883–1969), creator of *Gasoline Alley* comic strip; Cashton

Liberace (1919–1987), pianist; West Allis

Allen Ludden (1917–1981), *Password* host; Mineral Point

Alfred Lunt (1892–1977), actor and director; Milwaukee

Fredric March (1897–1975), actor (*The Best Years of Our Lives*); Racine

Jackie Mason (b. 1930), comedian; Sheboygan

Georgia O'Keeffe (1887–1986), painter; Sun Prairie

Les Paul (b. 1915), guitarist; Waukesha

Nicholas Ray (1911–1978), film director (*Rebel Without a Cause*); Galesville

Gena Rowlands (b. 1930), actress (*A Woman Under the Influence*); Cambria

Mona Simpson (b. 1957), novelist (*Anywhere But Here*); Green Bay

Tom Snyder (b. 1936), newscaster and talk-show host; Milwaukee

Gustav Stickley (1857–1942) Mission-style furniture designer; Osceola

Spencer Tracy (1900–1967), actor; Milwaukee

Thorstein Veblen (1857–1929), economist, social critic (*The Theory of the Leisure Class*); Manitowoc County

Orson Welles (1915–1985), actor, producer, director (*Citizen Kane*); Kenosha

...and Great Places

Some interesting derivations of Wisconsin place names.

Alaska Station Named for area's ice industry, which supplied Milwaukee breweries and local resorts.

Aztalan N. F. Hyer, who discovered remains of ancient city in Jefferson County, named the site in honor of Mexican Aztec legend about ancestors from the north.

Beetown Name comes from a 425-pound lead nugget found under a bee tree in 1827.

Belgium Name chosen by U.S. government after citizens requested "Luxembourg." "Luxemburg" was assigned to a town on the Door Peninsula, not far from Denmark, Poland, and Brussels.

Butte des Morts "Hill of the Dead," site of large number of Indian burials and reburials.

Couderay From Court Oreilles ("short ears"). French explorers thought Ojibwe in area had cut off part of their ears, a misunderstanding probably based on hairstyles or headgear.

Deronda At 1886 meeting to select town name, daughter of one of original settlers was reading George Eliot's *Daniel Deronda*.

Kenosha Potawatomi villages in area were called *kenosha*, meaning "pike" or "pickerel."

La Crosse Explorers saw Native Americans playing a game that resembled French sport of lacrosse, so named because the racquet resembled a bishop's crozier.

Maiden Rock A bluff overlooking the Mississippi River in Pierce County, named for a Sioux maiden who, according to legend, jumped to her death after being made to marry against her will.

Milwaukee Many old spellings and possible derivations exist; one likely meaning is "a gathering place by the river."

Prairie du Chien French for "Dog's Prairie." Local Fox chief was known as Dog.

Racine French word for "root." For the root-clogged river that made canoe traffic difficult.

Sheboygan Uncertain derivation from Indian words. Some meanings involve hollow objects such as pipe stems, reeds, or bones, or a tool for piercing. Others refer to a river that disappears underground or an underground noise.

Wisconsin Probably from Ojibwe *wees-kon-san* ("gathering of the waters") or Winnebago *wis-koos-er-ah* ("river of the flowering banks").

WISCONSIN BY THE SEASONS
A Perennial Calendar of Events and Festivals

*Here is a selective listing of events that take place each year in the months noted;
we suggest calling ahead to local chambers of commerce for dates and details.*

January

Lake Nebagamon
Fisharama
Ice-fishing contest on 950-acre lake.

Milwaukee
U.S. International Snow Sculpting Competition
Teams from all over the world participate.

White Lake
Snowshoe Rendezvous
Kids' treasure hunt, 5K run, fry pan toss, torchlight walk.

February

Cable/Hayward
Dyno American Birkebeiner
Premier cross-country ski races in North America.

Madison
Kites on Ice
Stunt flying, kite skiing, indoor and outdoor events.

Wausau
Special Olympics Winter Games
Statewide competition in skiing and skating.

March

Appleton
Adopt-a-Bucket

Do-it-yourself maple-sap collecting.

Madison
Canoecopia
World's largest paddle-sport exposition.

Nekoosa
Walleye Days
Three-week fishing tournament.

April

Burlington
Yo-Yo Convention and Contest
Exhibits, workshops, and original-trick competition, at Spinning Top Museum.

Milwaukee
Dinosaur Dash
5K walk/run through downtown streets; route runs through Milwaukee Public Museum.

Wisconsin Dells
Spring Polka Fest
Music, dancing, specialty foods in three venues.

May

Ashland
Scandinavian Heritage Day
Folk dancing, genealogy booth, Norwegian fjord horses.

Baraboo
Crane Fest
Birdhouse building, crane dancing, and lectures at the Crane Foundation.

Stevens Point
Spring Festival of Beers
Sampling of more than 100 craft-brewed beers; keg bowling.

Sturgeon Bay
Door County Lighthouse Walk
Walking tour of five mainland lighthouses; boat tours to others.

June

Coon Valley
Norskedalen's Midsummer Fest
Scandinavian festival celebrating the summer solstice.

Little Chute
Great Wisconsin Cheese Festival
Curd-eating contest, cheese carving, cheesecake contest.

Milwaukee
Summerfest
Thousands of performers participate in the world's biggest music festival.

Oshkosh
Miss Wisconsin Pageant Parade
Kickoff to statewide competition.

July

Cassville
Twin-o-Rama
Festival honoring twins and other multiples.

Elkhart Lake
Vintage International Challenge
Road America hosts the country's largest classic-car racing event.

Grantsburg
World Championship Snowmobile Watercross
Snowmobiles race on water.

Lac du Flambeau
Bear River Powwow
Social dancing, singing, food, crafts.

August

Cumberland
Rutabaga Festival
Cook-offs, tournaments, bike race, and parade.

Eagle River
National Championship Muskie Open
Anglers try to catch and release the biggest muskie.

West Allis
State Fair
Livestock judging, grandstand entertainment, cream puffs, and fireworks.

September

Apostle Islands
Lighthouse Celebration
Cruises and tours of seven historic lighthouses; lectures, dinner.

Hayward
Chequamegon Fat Tire Festival
Off-road bicycle fest with 16- and 40-mile cross-country events.

Mineral Point
Cornish Festival
Tours of town's historic district; Cornish food, storytelling, and entertainment.

New Glarus
Wilhelm Tell Festival
Swiss-themed entertainment, food, yodeling contest, performance of *Wilhelm Tell*.

October

Appleton
Halloween with Houdini
Magic show commemorating the Appleton-bred illusionist, who died on Halloween in 1926.

Coon Valley
Civil War Heritage Weekend
Encampment, skirmish, artillery drills, living-history demonstrations.

West Salem
Hmong New Year Festival
Music, dance, food, soccer tournament.

November

Tomahawk
Free Venison Feed
Thousands of venison burgers are served.

Waukesha
World's Greatest Cookie Sale
Large-scale bake sale for non-profit organizations.

West Allis
Train Fest
Midwest's largest model-train show, with more than 40 operating layouts.

December

Mayville
Heritage Fest
German winterfest with ice sculpture, showshoe races, beer tasting.

Merrimac
Snowboard Jam
Downhill and snowboarding competition.

Sheboygan Falls
Main Street Memories
Christmas carolers, carriage rides, bell choirs in historic town.

WHERE TO GO

Museums, Attractions, Gardens, and Other Arts Resources

Call for seasons and hours when open.

Museums

BADGER MINE MUSEUM
279 Estey St., Shullsburg, 608-965-4860
Exhibits on history of lead mining in southwestern Wisconsin.

CHARLES ALLIS ART MUSEUM
1801 N. Prospect Ave., Milwaukee, 414-278-8295
Fine art and furniture displayed in an elegant Tudor mansion.

CHARLES A. WUSTUM MUSEUM OF FINE ARTS
2519 Northwestern Ave., Racine, 414-636-9177
Twentieth-century American watercolors, photography, large collection of WPA artwork.

CIRCUS WORLD MUSEUM
426 Water St., Baraboo, 608-356-0800
More than 100 years' worth of circus memorabilia, at original headquarters of Ringling Brothers circus.

ELVEHJEM MUSEUM OF ART
800 University Ave., Madison, 608-263-2246
Permanent collections include Egyptian and Greek antiquities, Renaissance church art, Japanese prints, Russian icons, and early Americana.

GREAT LAKES COAST GUARD MUSEUM
2022 Jackson St., Two Rivers, 920-793-5905
Lighthouse-related artifacts, retired vessels, shipwreck memorabilia.

HOARD HISTORICAL MUSEUM
407 Merchants Ave., Fort Atkinson, 920-563-7769
Native American artifacts; also exhibits related to dairying (W. D. Hoard was instrumental in establishing state's dairy industry).

MADISON ART CENTER
211 State St., Madison, 608-257-0158
Contemporary and performance art, photography.

MADISON CHILDREN'S MUSEUM
100 State St., Madison, 608-256-6445
Hands-on and traditional exhibits and activities for kids.

MID-CONTINENT RAILWAY MUSEUM
West of Baraboo on WI 136 and CR PF, 608-522-4261
Operating steam engine, refurbished railroad coaches, cabooses, freight cars; 19th-century depot.

MILWAUKEE ART MUSEUM
750 N. Lincoln Memorial Dr., Milwaukee, 414-224-3200
Eero Saarinen designed the landmark building; collections are especially strong in German Expressionism, Haitian art, Frank Lloyd Wright material.

MILWAUKEE PUBLIC MUSEUM
800 W. Wells St., Milwaukee, 414-278-2700
Everything from dinosaur bones to IMAX, as well as archaeology, anthropology, geology, botany, and ethnography exhibits.

NATIONAL FRESHWATER FISHING HALL OF FAME
Off WI 27, on CR B, Hayward–Cable, 715-634-4440
Hundreds of mounted fish, antique rods and reels, 5,000 lures—all inside a four-story fiberglass muskie.

ONEIDA NATION MUSEUM
W892 EE Rd., Green Bay, 920-869-2768
Exhibits on Oneida history and culture; outdoor longhouse and stockade.

PESHTIGO FIRE MUSEUM
Oconto Ave., Peshtigo, 715-582-3244
Photos and artifacts that survived the devastating
1871 fire; museum is in old church, adjacent to
cemetery in which victims are buried.

RHINELANDER LOGGING MUSEUM
Just off Bus. 8, downtown Rhinelander, 715-369-5004
Old logging equipment and photos, displayed in
former logging camp dining hall.

STATE HISTORICAL MUSEUM
30 N. Carroll St., Madison, 608-264-6555
Exhibits on geological and Native American history;
bookstore strong on state history.

WEST BEND ART MUSEUM
300 S. 6th Ave., West Bend, 414-334-9638
Paintings by early 19th-century Wisconsin artists;
large antique dollhouse.

WISCONSIN MARITIME MUSEUM
75 Maritime Dr., Manitowoc, 920-684-0218
Re-creations of port towns and harborfronts, the
USS Cobia submarine, displays on early Great Lakes
shipping, model-ship gallery, nautical artifacts.

Attractions

CAVE OF THE MOUNDS
Blue Mound State Park
The cave, discovered in 1939, is considered the most
significant in the upper Midwest.

DICKEYVILLE GROTTO
305 W. Main St., Dickeyville
Religious and patriotic themes expressed in concrete
studded with glass, shells, tile, and other materials.

HOUDINI HISTORICAL CENTER
330 E. College Ave., Appleton, 920-735-8445
Comprehensive collection of photos and equipment
used by Houdini.

HOUSE ON THE ROCK
South of Spring Green along WI 23, 608-935-3639
Eccentricity writ large: oddball collection of antique
dolls, musical instruments, armor, carousel animals,
and much more.

MILWAUKEE COUNTY ZOO
10001 W. Bluemound Rd., Milwaukee, 414-771-3040
Mammals, birds, and reptiles presented in state-of-
the-art environments.

OLD WORLD WISCONSIN
Eagle, 414-594-2116
Large complex of distinctive structures from the early
days of immigration, brought here from all over the
state.

PENDARVIS
114 Shake Rag St., Mineral Point, 608-987-2122
Complex of restored Cornish cottages from the
town's lead- and zinc-mining days.

S. C. JOHNSON WAX ADMINISTRATION BUILDING
1525 Howe St., Racine, 414-631-2154
A Frank Lloyd Wright masterpiece of innovative
workplace design.

TALIESIN
Three miles south of Spring Green, 608-588-2361
Wright's rural retreat and studio.

WISCONSIN CONCRETE PARK
Hwy. 13, south of Phillips, 715-339-4505
About 200 concrete sculptures, mostly human and
animal figures—folk artist Fred Smith's magnum
opus.

WISCONSIN DELLS
800-22DELLS
Family-oriented attractions, souvenir shops, restaurants, rocks, and water.

Homes and Gardens

BOERNER BOTANICAL GARDEN
5879 S. 92nd St., Milwaukee, 414-425-1130
Fifty acres of formal gardens.

MITCHELL PARK HORTICULTURAL CONSERVATORY
524 S. Layton Ave., Milwaukee, 414-425-1130
Three domes house flowers and rain-forest and desert environments.

OLBRICH BOTANICAL GARDENS AND TROPICAL CONSERVANCY
3330 Atwood Ave., Madison, 608-246-4550
Indoor and outdoor horticultural displays.

PABST MANSION
2000 W. Wisconsin Ave., Milwaukee, 414-931-0808
Capt. Frederick Pabst's 37-room residence, built in 1890–93 in Flemish Renaissance style, in Milwaukee's distinctive cream-colored brick.

UNIVERSITY OF WISCONSIN ARBORETUM
1207 Seminole Hwy., Madison, 608-263-7888
Native plants, deciduous forest; wetlands and prairies restored to pre-settlement conditions.

VILLA LOUIS
521 Villa Louis Road, Prairie du Chien, 608-326-2721
Lavishly appointed 1870s Italianate mansion built by son of Wisconsin's first millionaire, fur trader Hercules Dousman.

WINGSPREAD
33 E. Four Mile Rd., Wind Point, 414-639-3211
Once the private residence of H. F. (Johnson Wax) Johnson, this is the largest and last Prairie-style house designed by Frank Lloyd Wright, completed in 1937.

Other Resources

DOOR COUNTY CHAMBER OF COMMERCE
P.O. Box 406
Sturgeon Bay, WI 54235
800-52RELAX
www.doorcountyvacations.com

GREATER MADISON CONVENTION AND VISITORS BUREAU
615 E. Washington Ave.
Madison, WI 53703
800-373-6376
www.visitmadison.com

GREATER MILWAUKEE CONVENTION AND VISITORS BUREAU
510 W. Kilbourn Ave.
Milwaukee, WI 53203
800-554-1448
www.milwaukee.org/visit.htm

WISCONSIN DEPARTMENT OF TOURISM
201 W. Washington Ave.
P.O. Box 7976
Madison, WI 53707
800-432-8747
www.travelwisconsin.com

CREDITS

The authors have made every effort to reach copyright holders of text and owners of illustrations, and wish to thank those individuals and institutions that permitted the reprinting of text or the reproduction of works in their collections. Credits not listed in the captions are provided below. References are to page numbers; the designations a, b, and c indicate position of illustrations on pages.

Text

Lorine Niedecker: Copyright ©1985, 1996 by the Estate of Lorine Niedecker, Cid Corman, executor.

Illustrations

COLLECTION OF MR. AND MRS. JOHN BOLZ: **8** *Harvest Time,* 1944. Oil on canvas. 26 x 21½"; D. P. BURNSIDE/PHOTO RESEARCHERS: **87a;** COLLECTION MARK AND SIGRID CULLICKSON: **31** *Reclining Herd,* 1962. Casein on paper. 35 x 23"; CULVER PICTURES: **29b** *Great Fire at Peshtigo,* 1871. Woodcut; **88;** ELVEHJEM MUSEUM OF ART, UNIVERSITY OF WISCONSIN: **2** *Wisconsin Farm Scene,* 1941. Oil on canvas. 88¹³⁄₁₆ x 97". Gift of First National Bank and First Wisconsin Corp, 1985; DANIEL GERHARTZ: **1** *Evening Holsteins,* 1997. Oil on canvas. 18 x 30"; LAYNE KENNEDY/CORBIS: **87b;** J. M. KOHLER ART CENTER: **81** *Statues in Hollandale Yard.* Oil on masonite. 15⅞ x 34¼"; **85a** *Carved and Mosaic Sculptures,* 1960–80. Mixed media. Collection of Mary Nohl; MADISON ART CENTER: **46b** *Progressive Party Rally,* 1938. Oil on canvas. 11½ x 15½". Gift of family of Philip and Isabel LaFollette; THE METROPOLITAN MUSEUM OF ART: **19** *Wisconsin Landscape,* 1938–39. Oil on canvas. 42 x 84". George A. Hearn Fund, 1942. Copyright 1981; MILWAUKEE ART MUSEUM: **11** Wood, paint, metal. 5¾ x 17⅜ x 6". Michael and Julie Hall Collection of American Folk Art; **54** *Ice Fishing, Lake Mendota,* 1949. Oil on masonite. 18 x 24⅛". Gift of Gimbel Brothers. © Estate of Aaron Bohrod/Licensed by VAGA, N.Y.; **76** *View of the Fox River,* 1885–88. Oil on canvas. 26⅛ x 31¼". Gift of friends of the artist; **77** *A Veil of Snow,* 1910. Oil on canvas. 24¹⁄₁₆ x 31". Gift of 12 Friends; **78** *Main Street, Alma,* 1925. Oil on board. 15⅞ x 19⅞". Gift of friends and of Men's Sketch Club in honor of Gustave Moeller; MUSEUM OF WOODCARVING: **83a** Photo by V. Eric Jensen; NATIONAL GEOGRAPHIC IMAGE COLLECTION: **12a** Marilyn Dye Smith; **12b** Robert E. Hynes; NATIONAL MUSEUM OF AMERICAN ART, SMITHSONIAN INSTITUTION: **79a** *Autumn Field,* 1957. Tempera on paper. 119.4 x 91.5 cm; **79b** *Happy, Crazy American Animals and a Man and Lady at My Place,* 1961. Gift of S. C. Johnson and son; COURTESY RINGLING BROS.–BARNUM &BAILEY COMBINED SHOWS, INC.: **63a** Ringling Bros. is a registered trademark of Ringling Bros.–Barnum & Bailey Combined Shows, Inc. All rights reserved; STATE HISTORICAL SOCIETY OF WISCONSIN: **16; 17; 38b; 45b; 59b;** WEST BEND ART MUSEUM: **33** *Dry Dock,* 1998. Watercolor and gouache. 17½ x 27⅜"; ZANE WILLIAMS: **21b; 49c; 80; 82; 83b; 86a; 86b; 89;** WISCONSIN ACADEMY GALLERY: **84** *Phantom Buck II,* 2000. Oil on canvas. 24 x 32"; **85b** *Nin Minwendamia,* 1999. Oil on canvas. 44¼ x 47"; COURTESY WRIGHT MUSEUM OF ART, BELOIT COLLEGE: **44** *Dewy Morning,* n.d. Oil on canvas. 25 x 32". Gift of Helen Brace Emerson

Acknowledgments

Grateful thanks are extended to Elizabeth Schmoeger, Milwaukee Art Museum; Lonni Lown and Jim Nidy; Lynne Eich, director, Dane County Cultural Affairs Commission; and Randall E. Berndt, director, Wisconsin Academy Gallery.